Plants for Dinner

Becca Heddle

Explorer Challenge

Find out what part
of the plant this is ...

OXFORD

UNIVERSITY PRESS

In this book you will see ✅ and ❌ on plants.

✅ is for plants that are food

❌ is for plants that are not food

Contents

Plants for Dinner 4

Roots 6

Stems 8

Leaves 10

Buds and Flowers 12

Fruit 14

Seeds 16

Shoots 18

Parts of Plants 20

Glossary and Index 22

Look Back, Explorers 23

Plants for Dinner

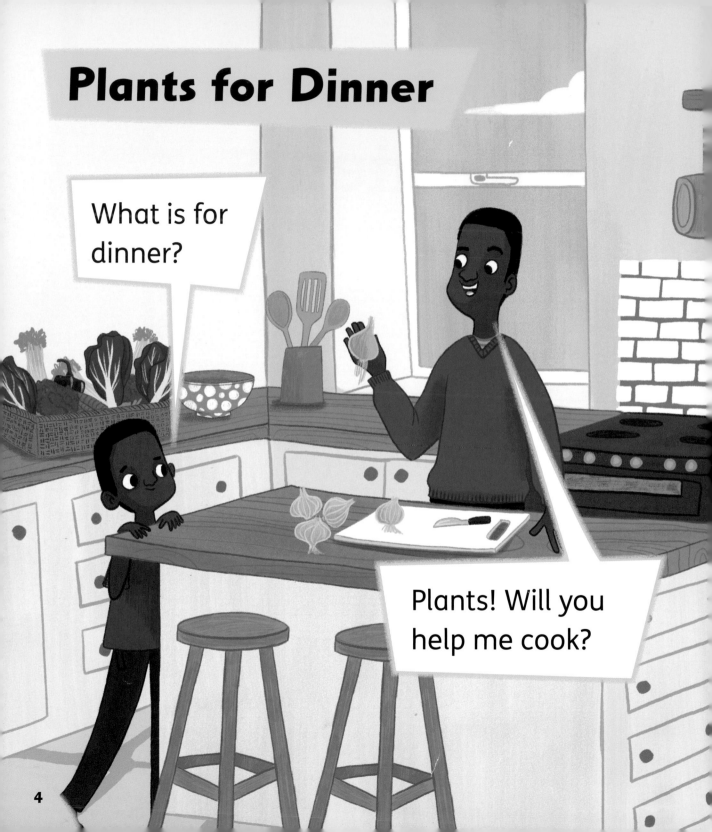

Plants are fantastic, from the roots to the top. Come and see!

5

Roots

Roots go down into the soil. They can grow thick.

Carrots are roots.

thin roots

tree roots

7

A tree's trunk is its stem.

thin flower stems

long bamboo stems

9

Leaves

Plants have leaves. There are lots of different sorts of leaves.

thin, soft leaves

fat, stiff leaves

leaves with sharp points

11

Buds and Flowers

Flowers grow from flower buds. The flowers of different plants look and smell different.

Some buds are green.

This flower smells horrid!

This flower smells sweet.

13

Fruit

Lots of plants have **fruit**. Lemons, plums, peppers and pumpkins are all fruit.

All fruits have seeds in them.

Seeds

Lots of plants have **seeds**. Seeds can be in **pods**, **nuts** or in fruit. Seeds can grow into new plants.

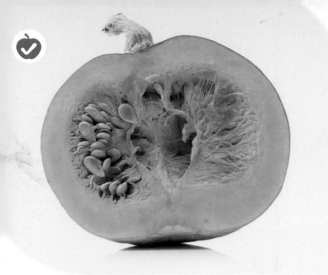

pod with seeds

fruit with seeds

nut

seed

Shoots

A shoot grows from a seed. It is the start of a new plant.

cress shoot

seed

19

Parts of Plants

We will have lots of parts of plants for dinner.

Fruit, flower buds, roots, stems, seeds, shoots and leaves. Yum!

Glossary

fruit: part of some plants with seeds in; some fruits are food

nuts: part of some plants with a hard shell and a seed or seeds in; some nuts are food

pods: part of some plants with seeds in; some pods are food

seeds: little parts of plants that can grow into new plants; some seeds are food

Index

fruit   14–15, 16, 17, 21
plants   4–5, 8, 10, 12, 14, 16, 18, 20
roots   5, 6–7, 21
seed   15, 16–17, 18, 19, 21

Look Back, Explorers

At the end of the book, the boy says 'Yum!' What other words mean the same as *yum*?

Can you name a fruit?

Where do plant shoots grow from?

Imagine you are joining the boy and his dad for dinner. What questions would you ask them about what they are cooking?

Did you find out what part of the plant this is?

Explorer Challenge: the flower buds (page 13)

What's Next, Explorers?

Now that you know about
different parts of plants,
go on a magic key
adventure to hunt for a
smelly flower ...

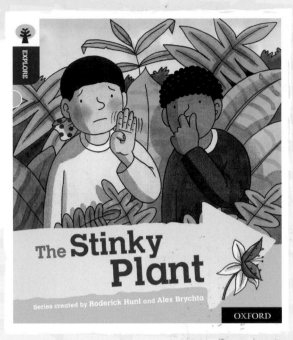

The Stinky Plant

Series created by Roderick Hunt and Alex Brychta

OXFORD

Explorer Challenge
for *The Stinky Plant*

Find out what
eats the fruit ...